Better than
Paradise

Better than Paradise
Will Holloway

Smokestack Books
1 Lake Terrace, Grewelthorpe, Ripon HG4 3BU
e-mail: info@smokestack-books.co.uk
www.smokestack-books.co.uk

ISBN 9781999827625

Smokestack Books
is represented
by Inpress Ltd

To Brenna

Contents

III. World Maps (Folded)

I
Embryo Concepts

Were the beautiful volute and cone shells of the Eocene epoch, and the gracefully sculptured ammonites of the Secondary period, created that man might ages afterwards admire them in his cabinet?

Charles Darwin, *On the Origin of Species*, 1859

Creation Song of the Indigenous People of the Puedam Region

The World began in light
and the light was very great
but there was as yet no eye to see,
no spirit to look,
and no creation to be seen.
And so the World began in darkness.

The World began in din
and the din was terrible and lovely
but there was as yet no ear to hear,
no spirit to listen,
and no word to be spoken.
And so the World began in silence.

On the face of the darkness was only light
and in the space of the light there was only darkness.
Within the din was only silence
and without the silence there was only senseless din.

And the World was very small in those times,
much smaller than its smallest part is now.

But between the darkness and the light,
there at last came twilight and early dawn,
there came gloom and there came shade.
And between the silence and the din,
there came a hum,
there came roar and whistle and rustle and buzz.
And so it came to pass
that the woman and the man
spoke words to one another in the garden.

I Did Not Speak Out

First they came for the Jews
but I did not speak out
because I am an Artist
and I don't want to turn what I do
into mere propaganda.

Then they built gigantic missiles,
enough to destroy the Earth,
but I did not speak out
because Art is interested
only in what is eternal.

Then they dried the wells of a nation
and drowned the thirsty who fled
but I did not speak out
because Literature is about
the intricate paradoxes of the heart,

in other words: adultery amongst the intelligentsia.
History is rising in waves but
Poetry is on the beach, shouting:
Back, waves, go back!
I command you!

Knickers on Frogs

for Lazzaro Spallanzani

My enemies have accused me of stealing monsters.
A visitor noticed my embryos in jars,
the two-headed foal, the surprised homunculi,
and also noticed the labels 'University of Pavia'
and reported the matter to the Dean.

No one said science was easy, for instance
if I was going to put rubber knickers
on any animal for fun,
frogs would be my last choice.
The combination of slippery and good-at-jumping
easy out-inconveniences
the dog (truculent) or even the spider (fiddly).

One can only imagine the farcical scenes
in Reaumur's laboratory, frogs wriggling free
from his gloved hands, jumping across the room,
crossing in mid-air like acrobats,
startling him with an unexpected croak,
an eye suddenly magnified behind the glassware,
a tongue flickers, an idiosyncratic thermometer is smashed
and the frog, once dressed, clawing at its trews,
peeling them back, elbowing itself naked,
the great man cursing in the Atlantic dialect of his boyhood.

Well really, professor, you must persevere.
Consider the frogs themselves.
See how the sire jiggles his lass,
hiccupping the milt from his hips,
slathering it across her backside
in sloppy gurgles of amphibian bliss.

I've secateured his legs off in the act
but he's undistractable. What a king!
He just clasps her all the tighter in his arms,
as single minded as I am in proving
that when frogs wear pants there are no tadpoles,
that frogs are caused by frogs fucking,
a fact which, like all great revelations,
creates a new age in which it seems entirely obvious.

Frogspawn is not created
spontaneously by some vital spirit.
The bare Earth gives no milk.

Life is not created at all
but transmitted by existing life,
through the action of particles,
tiny but solid enough to be thwarted
by a simple rubber barrier.

I have proved it,
succeeded where the Frenchman failed,
made nature a science,
cast out magic from the human mind,
murdered superstition in its bed,
and been dismissed from the University.

I have no need to steal monsters.
The label, you see, is not the thing.
I used stationery from work, that's all.
Fools! It was the labels I took, only the labels.

The So-Called Individual

for Rudolf Virchow

The first clue: cork through a lens is full of boundaries
Gentlemen, whilst bidding you heartily welcome
　　(The heron is its limbs, folding)

Telling the doctors the new news, passing round the slides
what the individual is on a grand scale,
the cell is that, and perhaps even more, on a small one
　　(The city is its citizens, quarrelling)

Appropriately, the theory emerged from many discoverers
existences are mutually dependent but in such a way
that every element has its own special action
　　(My fist is my hand, clenching)

Not only between ape and angel but between nucleus and nation
nothing has penetrated less deeply into the minds of all
than the cell-theory in its intimate connection with pathology
　　(I make, and am made by,
　　my parts and what I'm part of)

Implying the influence of public sanitation on private capillaries
I shall have no particular reason to justify myself, if in this respect,
I make quite a special reservation in favour of life
　　(The river is its droplets, passing)

The micrographs like eyes staring back, garish and diseased
disturbances which arise from social and political institutions,
and are therefore preventable
　　(My mind is my brain, feeling)

Plants, animals and impresarios, all made of the same
a body of considerable size, a so-called individual,
always represents a kind of social arrangement of parts
   (The world is a verb, elaborating)

Embryos growing into excitable microscopists
I am somewhat proud of having always,
in spite of the reproach of pedantry, firmly adhered to it
   (I'm not my cells,
    I'm what they do)

Your Fabulous Apartment

for Brenna

After the first operation
you knew the tumour would come back.
That was when you told me your dream

that you had to leave Los Angeles
and the black bean burritos
and the Frida Kahlo dresses at the Mexican market
and the shiatsu job and the clients.

Those clients! – you said –
They think it's totally usual to have dyed green pubes
but unbelievably weird to not own a car.

In the dream you had to go
and live in a huge, black, featureless skyscraper
in a huge, white, featureless desert.
It was the worst thing that had ever happened

but it had the best view.
The apartment was just fabulous
and looking out on one side
you could see every detail of L.A.

and on the other side you could see
all your friends from when you were in London
and they were all 25 again,
partying like idiots in a painted squat.

Those squatters! – you said –
As full of life and cider as apples on a tree,
ripening and ready to fall.

Transmigrants

So this new graduate was telling me their job
was demanding, away from home so often.
Turned out the job was: testing holidays
for a television programme.
Someone's got to do it.
It brings (vicarious) pleasure to millions.

This is what policymakers mean by social mobility.
They are secret reincarnationists.
The refugee is drowned only to live again,
born into a higher caste,
testing holidays on the same beach.

Mission Creep

The guard room always smelt of rain.
We wrote on the wall, soldiers' jokes.
We'd walk down to the village,
buy bread from the red-haired girls.

By the time the orders came,
we'd stopped walking back.
The roads are heathered over
but the wall is endless.

I take the grandchildren to see it.
They don't believe I was a Roman,
a word from a fairy tale, and even I
can't remember who it was
we were trying to keep out.

Gulls

The world is a great palace
of beaches, souvenirs and mini-golf.
I am too tiny to hurt it.
You can't crack the sky.

The lightswitch is full of light.
The airport is full of air,
circulating above me,
for a mile, for more, forever,

so space must be full of warm breezes
on which moths fly, hypnotised,
to the moth-coloured Moon.
Everywhere is exactly like home.

Smoke rises, thins, and is gone.
We do harmless ordinary things.
One day our grandchildren will do them too.
You can't crack the sky.

Gulls yap between the planets.
Passenger jets don't drop bombs.
The waitresses in the hotel restaurant smile
because they like me.

Parakeets

A squabble of branches overhead,
as if birds hadn't got the hang of trees yet,
resolves itself into a perfect arc,
a flashing locus of highlighter lime,

and the parakeet is in the next tree,
reassembling itself from the elbows out,
brandishing its ruby choker,
the gaudy anti-sparrow, the pirate's familiar,
the preening princeling of the poopdeck,
so un-English it's downright London.

Two toes forwards, two toes back,
it contains all its earlier drafts:

the last common ancestor of parakeet and duck,
surreptitiously dabbling in the shadows of dragons;

of parakeet and crocodile,
jewel-skinned whiptail,
sloping round the prehistoric pot plants;

of parakeet and monkey,
a toad-necked skulker,
sighing over its leathery eggs and dreaming,
in its black swamp, of its various children,
stowed on ramshackle galleons
or studying one another in sunlit surprise
in a future Kensington.

And instantly there's a whole flock,
pure mathematics across the sky,
pure vandalism in the foliage,
braying like betrayal,
blithely pivoting wingtips around
the wild blunders of history.

5.4 Million

because I had the World Service on at 2 a.m.
because I wondered what other enormities I'd missed
because I'd had time to get to page 17 of the paper
because the train was delayed by signal failure at Arnos Grove

because the soldiers took the crops and the village had nothing
because Human Immunodeficiency Virus is a weapon of war
because the children were in the accident at the coltan mine
because none of these people were there on their gap year

because there's a speck of Congo soil in every pocket in London
because two presidents were shot down in one plane crash
because America's creature wasted the country but saved the uranium
because Belgium divided and ruled by dividing hands from forearms

because the computer shop paid the electronics company
who paid the mining firm, who paid the armed faction
because of niobium, tantalum, copper, cadmium and manganese
because the entire periodic table is under threat

because indifference is an equal opportunities employer
because of coltan's capacity to store electric charge
because if this doesn't shock me, I've lost the capacity
and because in the darkness my laptop's screen
is shining like a lampshade

that's why there are five point four million dead people in this poem.

Victory to the Human League

I'm an environmentalist,
I like to see nature triumph
but not underneath my fridge.

I'm a vegan,
I don't like to hurt animals
except animals that try to eat my vegan food.

A cockroach is not an individual,
it's a message saying: your life has failed,
you live in infested squalor,
in a humid slum, a burnt-out derrie,
it's come to this: the insect house,
your dreams have led you only to Roach Motel
the roaches check in but they never check out
and all your exes will weep for what you have become because
a cockroach is not an individual,
it's the vanguard of an invading army from No. 76.

A routine patrol in the bathroom cupboard
engaged six unlawful combatants at twenty two hundred hours,
chemical weapons were deployed,
there were no survivors
but still they come.

My transformation is more Heinlein than Kafka,
I am like the Starship Troopers who cannot fight the swarm
without developing a carapace and a totalitarian hive mind.
We become the very arthropods that we oppose

so I have enlisted the help of a superpower whose chemical weapons
are immeasurably superior to my own –
I have formed a Human League with Islington Council

against the appalling efficiency of those antennae;
against the unnerving precision of the placing of their feet;
against the loathsome alertness of their posture,
the back sloping upwards, head high
like a gundog sniffing the wetland prospect;
against the prudent skitter and the cautious re-emergence
from the skirting as perhaps their apparent intelligence
emerges from the unswerving application of simple rules:
eat, walk, flee the bathroom light,
hold still when shadows are moving.

Just as the random drift of molecules is enough
to allow a poison gas to fill a room,
so a four-rule algorithm is enough
to allow a simple lucifuge to defeat
all the enlightenment of consciousness.
They are the shit-nibbling enemies of thought
whose implacable mindlessness is more terrifying
than any plan.

In the coal forests they were fierce, the size of rats,
but their lungless bodies were slow to take in oxygen.
Giant dragonflies clattered through the air like brass toys
but our ancestors had the gift of sudden movement,
the amphibious splash into the swamp,
the sinuous dart of backbone while stupid lobster
was still struggling to turn round.
So we were better at being our size but down there
on the centimetre level
there are microclimates beneath the bathmat
where the Palaeozoic never ended.

They can slide through holes so small
that the world is transparent, porous.
They no more notice the legal boundaries of my tenancy
than a migrating swallow notices
the hard borders of the European Union.

They are gathering beside the boiler.
They have discovered the hole in the grouting around the outflow.
They have reconnoitred the crumbs in the grill pan.
They know when I sleep and when I go out.
There is someone else here.
This is an old enmity.
We are not alone.

II
Democratic Ventriloquism

... I still think it's worth everything to say what you believe. There are always consequences and one must be prepared to face them. In this context there is no free speech and there never will be.

Andrea Dworkin, *Heartbreak:*
The Political Memoir of a Feminist Militant, 2002

Europe after the Rain

after Max Ernst

They thought the world was just five miles high,
eight thousand miles wide and six thousand years deep.
On the great shore of time
they refused to look outside their little beach hut.

They didn't believe in the coal forests,
the deserts of Pangaea or the Ice Ages.
They thought everything was fixed, a given.
They didn't believe in evolution or climate change
and so the world was, paradoxically,
destroyed by creationists.

Astonishingly, some of them did see it coming
but the Chicken Lickens didn't want
to jeopardise their credibility by sounding apocalyptic
so they confined themselves to warning only
of a significant risk of a reduction in celestial altitude.

It was an unfortunate law of human discourse
that the more pressing a problem
the more tedious you were to mention it;
importance made it daunting,
like an offputtingly fat Victorian novel.

They were doomed by social embarrassment
and by the Animist Theory of Technology, their belief
that there's an angel in the capital,
that the umbrella wants to shelter,
the gun to wants to terrify
and the turbine wants to generate.

They didn't invent tools to do their will,
they decided their will by feeling the heft
of the tools to hand,

so they raged on behalf of their cars,
ventriloquising the implicit opinions of their machines,
and became incapable of resisting their aeroplanes'
fathomless desire to be somewhere else,

until finally it wasn't the climate,
it wasn't the crop failures, hurricanes and diseases
but the wars they fought over their flooded ruins
that gave us our chance.

And now that we have decoded their books
and laid our eggs in their corpses
we must resolve, my fellow cockroaches,
not to make the same mistakes ourselves.

Mariolatrous in Antwerp

(Rubens, *The Assumption of the Holy Virgin*)

Anyone can see the category error,
the absurd mixture of material and spiritual:
up she rises
into heaven from her deathbed
and in all the wild confusion of the Counterreformation
she's accidentally taking the duvet with her.

Precisely what makes this ridiculous to us
is what made it credible to them:
that Rubens shows her
assumption not as a resonant metaphor
but as the adventure of some familiar,
rosy-fleshed, sensuous Dutchgirl
as literal and undeniably solid as a thigh bone,

so that he makes of this unbiblical,
baroque, cherub-chased beaming up
a mystery only as unlikely
as the presence of a beholder behind eyes,
a mind in a body,
a profane heart in a damp cathedral,
as my adoration of you
being quite literally expressed
through my own little incarnation.

Wine Crucifix

after Arnulf Rainer

Blood is a lively little wine
with a peach blossom nose
and surprisingly astringent cigar notes in the finish.

I drank 961 centilitres of alcohol altogether,
in 2007. I've kept detailed records
of the exact degree to which I lost control:
the equivalent of 102 bottles of red,
or 20 medium-sized priests.
Not much of a stain on the soul.
Not even a small share in a large invasion.

The people are nothing,
just cartoon faces in a noisy bar.
Only the wine is holy,
a coagulation spattering even the frame.

The torture isn't the torture,
the torture is the nightmares afterwards.
The chest scar is clamped open, again,
but the surgeon is suddenly mawkish.
The light shines on the altarpiece,
so that the cross is a shadow, sunless.
The Lionheart invents a flag with two wipes
of Arab gore on his white tunic.

And I must be the drunkest man in heaven.

Black Sites

You called me: Evil Empire.
It was partly through your expertise
in name-calling that you overcame me.

I was an archipelago within a fortress.
I was a state within a prison.
I was the remote Tartar city at which the prisoners
on the eastbound trains were unchained,
rationally, since beyond that point
there was nowhere to escape to
and the chains were sorely needed back west.

In those days the frenzy of my purges
and the torpor of my bureaucracy sometimes cancelled out,
a pianist released before interrogation
because the interrogator had himself been taken.

I taught that my victory was inevitable,
that the Slow War was my patient way
of placing the entire planet under arrest.

You won that war but the spirit of the conquered
seeps into the conqueror.
The Norman invader becomes a fastidious Englishman;
the brutal Ostrogoth, an Italian fop.

And so the 3 a.m. knock is heard again,
this time, as planned, inevitably,
across the housing estates of Western Europe.
The extraordinary renditions have just begun.
Those suspected of contacts with atrocitists
are removed by non-existent persons
to non-existent places.

Your hard-won oil is oiling the locks
at my old camps, at the Black Sites.

I am yours now.
Our great days are ahead.

Are we not all, in a sense…

They do not mate with the Queen.
They do not march against wars
in Waziristan. They do not fly home
in drone-shaped coffins
with their little wings poking out the sides.
Their mums never appear on television complaining
that they should have been given better tailfins.

If you cut them, they do not bleed.
They do not spend their R and R having poon tang
with self-service Sainsbury's tills.

They are not internally displaced persons
fleeing in their thousands across the South Downs.
They have not established a beachhead
on page 17 of the better papers.
They did not become complicit just by pressing Send.

They are not client states,
they are not private sector subcontractors
but they are, as a metaphor, always accurate
because everything is a target.

They are not disarmingly frank at the press conference.
They do not worry if that was the wrong house.
They do not know that death
is only the beginning of grieving.

They should have been careful
what they wished for.
They are not solely used
for delivering spice to D wing.
They do not have an exit,
or any other, strategy
and drones, as requested,
are not in our name.

The Fall of the Crown

King George I
King John I
King Thomas
King James I
King James II
King John II
King Andrew I
King Martin
King William I
King John III
King James III
King Zachary
King Millard
King Franklin I
King James IV
King Abraham
King Andrew II
King Ulysses
King Rutherford
King James V
King Chester
King Grover
King Benjamin
King William II
King Theodore
King William III
King Woodrow
King Warren
King Calvin
King Herbert
King Franklin II
King Harold
King Dwight
King John IV
King Lyndon

King Richard
King Gerald
King James VI
King Ronald
King George II
King William IV
King George III
King Barack
King Donald

Michael the First

I didn't kneel on the floor,
getting glue in my hair, I sat
at the table, smoothing the newsprint
in my Kennedy scrapbook.

No one would choose to be different,
not that I'm a bigot but
there are bigots out there
and who would want to face them?

Lunatics are tremendous people.
They give you the presents you wanted
but couldn't ask for. Plus
you can call the doctor.

It's like one of those classic what-ifs:
if presidents were chosen like juries.
I'm the tenth accident: four bullets, a heart attack,
a stroke, cholera, a nasty cold, a burglary and now

this mess, which can be tidied. We've been
in dubious company and we need to
come home, be cured, sit up straight
and keep our scissors clean.

This 2017 and No Other

The other me, or rather mes,
in other worlds are dining out
with their astounding parallel universe girlfriend.
I might've studied, moved to Boston
to wear a shirt like a lumberjack,
married the one I got away from.

It was a vote that seemed to asking:
Do you like what you're getting?
Obviously we said No and now we find
that the Godzilla administration's fiery breath is
certainly a refreshing approach to urban planning.

As soon as our feet weren't hands
we stood up on them and migrated
right out of the Olduvai Gorge.

It's called social housing because it's very social
that the neighbours are on fire too.

Alternatively: the new arrivals have fled
southwards across the sea from civil war
and drizzle to the reception centre
outside El Fayum. They have lost their identity
documents but are adamant that they were blue.

You can't blame the Tories for everything.
It's not Iain Duncan Smith
pisses in the lift on our estate.
Although it is, in a way.

If you were sucked through time,
how would you make a living?
My detailed knowledge of the tax system
is completely useless even in another country.
Who is safe from this kind of temporal vortex de-skilling?
Only barbers and maths teachers.

Back then you could visit the Empire,
massacre colonials and get a tower named after you
that goes on fire and massacres
the colonials' descendants.

Dreams are real, they're visions
from moments in other lives
where the background music coincides.

I like disturbing coulda woulda shoulda realities
where Kensington has turned into Aleppo
but I wish they'd stay in the boxed set.

My grandmother needs an English class please.
She is fresh out of tunnel and my people
need a homeland, somewhere we can be in peace
and sell distinctive pastries though, if I'm honest bruv,
Kilburn would not have been our first choice.

Renters used to die in secret of bad boilers
not in a flagrant torch illuminating the whole city.
It could be the emblem on the national flag
of what it's created: like Year Ten bunking
to organise the volunteer food distributors.

And I ask you today, sisters and brothers,
can anyone amongst us truly say
that they are not migrating
towards or away from a flatulent middle age?
In and out of the inky rock pools of dream?

Far from the Karoo sandstone beds,
ever westwards around the galactic centre?

Poverty is unsightly so they put up a facade
but it was the facade that caught light.

Life has film music, you're swept along
without noticing: Jeopardy! Gloom! Love!
And a man in a rubber lizard suit
menacing a train set.

And about my other life,
the thing I was going to say,
it escapes me
or me, it.

Misdirection

I'm transfixed by him
which might be the point,
that he is the glamorous assistant.

The audience cannot stop pointing out
his unusual gestures,
locution, hairdo and Twitter style.

But his genius at inarticulacy
is nothing but his sequinned leotard
distracting me while the magician
disappears my watch.

Our Chairman

A revolution is not a dinner party

It's little known fact that
before the Long March came the Long Tour

it's not painting a picture, ladies & gentlemen,
an it's not writing a dissertation

before his gruelling conquest of China
Mao Zedong endured an equally gruelling
stint on the Northern club circuit

behave yourself madam,
it's not anything like that at all,
a revolution is an act of violence
by which one class brays another

and it was there that he first honed down
the collection of one-liners
later to become famous as the 'Thoughts'

an I'll tell you another thing, them imperialists,
they're rum buggers, aren't they?
I said behave yourself madam.

Tonight: The Great Pedanto

I am the microscope observed.
I am science hunched over its bench
and photographed, caught in the act of gazing in.

I am my precise ingredients
from my feet to my stage forceps,
in transmitted or incident light.
I am the great pedant, the devourer of detail.

I have counted the angels
on the head of the pin
and then counted the pins
holding up the hems of their frocks.

I am the optical diagram
of the paths of rays through objective lenses,
where each dotted line is a scalpel
separating the whole into its parts.

By magnifying, I reduce to simple elements.
By dividing I unite;
plants and animals, chorus girls and impresarios,
are all made of the same cells
with the same fine contraptions inside.

I'm top of the bill.
I've performed my act.
I've taken myself to pieces
and laid them out for your audience in their millinery
to gasp at, then wonder
how all the pieces
are ever going to fit back together.

Disaster Movie

(Goya, *El Coloso*)

You don't need to see the giant to see the giant,
just project the lines of refugees backwards
and there's his colossal arse, massively indifferent
to the boy falling from the horse,
the woman in the mud.

But you have to see the painting to see the painting:
the individual daubs like the crests of waves,
the terrible grime on his upper arm,
you project the movement backwards,
you see them being painted.

The Colossus is a verb,
he's almost left the picture,
Goya was too slow,
as humans are when
we injure ourselves in flight,
wagons broken forever,
cities just empty stones.

In the sky a glance at his face
is the only light against the geological dusk.
And if he leaves
he's still implied by everything else.
You don't need to see the giant,
he is the cataclysm behind the trees,
behind the clouds.

III
World Maps (Folded)

'Tis not like the ascension of a vapour to the sky; nay, but like the ascension of an embryo to rationality.

Rumi, *The Spiritual Ascension*
(translated by R.A. Nicholson, *Rumi*, 1950)

Turtles

The Glastonbury Version

I saw the Universe
and it looked a lot like foam
but the walls of the bubbles
were sheets of hundreds of superclusters of galaxies
and the bubbles themselves were voids,
empty spaces 150 million light years across,
because the biggest things there are
are nothings.

And I looked a thousand times closer
and somewhere between the Fornax Void
and the Corona Borealis Void,
like a peninsula sticking out
from one end of the Centaurus Supercluster,
I saw the Virgo Supercluster
in all its splendour and intricacy.
I saw that it was made of smaller clusters
of spiral galaxies and dwarf irregulars
and their haloes of dark matter.

And I looked a thousand times closer
and in one of those smaller clusters I saw
the second of three great spirals, a turning city
of two hundred thousand million stars
with its spiral arms lazily, fuzzily
wrapped around its glowing core.

And I looked a thousand times closer
and in one of those arms, in the Orion arm,
I saw a small region of just about a thousand stars
and some were bright and white and fast-burning
and some were dim red dwarfs
and some were moderate and yellow.

And I looked a thousand times closer
and I saw one star screaming out
its yellow light into empty space.

And I looked a thousand times closer,
so closely that I could see the star's innermost planets,
four spinning balls of rock
and an asteroid belt rich in minerals.

And I looked a thousand times closer
and I saw one of the planets and its moon.
And the planet was blue and swirly
and its moon was dotted with American flags
    being perhaps the only American conquest
    never to have fought back.

And I looked a thousand times closer
and on the planet's surface,
just off the northwest coast of its largest land mass,
I saw a group of rainy islands.

And I looked a thousand times closer
and on one of the islands
I saw a large concentration of people, a bit like a city
but with fewer buildings and more falafels.
I saw muddy lanes and giant tents and amplifier stacks
and incense and dayglo wellies.

And I looked a thousand times closer
and in one of the dirtier tents,
standing on a stage in front of an audience of shining eyes,
I saw a man talking
about the huge and silent, explosive, whirling
galaxies all around him.

And I looked a thousand times closer
and I saw a single cubic millimetre of the grey goo of his brain,
still as stone
but to him alive with thoughts
about how his voice was sounding through the microphone
and whether he'd be able to finish the overlong last line of the verse without
breathing.

And I looked a thousand times closer
and I saw a nerve cell in that brain
firing a little jolt of electricity to the next nerve cell
    as part of some long, vague thought
    about a neurophilosopher's claim
    that Emergence is only a word
    which restates the obvious truth
    that the complex qualities of things
    emerge from their simplest details,
    that sharpness is a characteristic
    of neither side of the blade
    but rather of the whole knife,
    that the word is a semantic elastoplast
    on the wound of our ignorance
    which, had you observed the Universe from a safe distance,
    wouldn't have helped you predict the emergence
    of life or of mind
    or of whatever's going to emerge next.

And so I looked a thousand times closer.
I saw the nucleus of the nerve cell.
I saw its chromosomes and their coils within coils.
I saw the twisted ladder of DNA and within that
a single rung, a base pair.

And I thought: Anyone who could reorder these rungs
        could control what emerges:
        the firing of synapses in the brain;
        the flight of the bumblebee;
        the shelf life of the tomato;
        the wrinkles in the human face;
        the weeds in the fields of India
        and the livelihoods of the farmers of the world.

And when I saw genes being manipulated like that,
when I saw biotechnology,
I thought: That's so cool
        but what if it doesn't work?
        What if it breeds out of control?
        What if the virus hits the grain silos?
        What if the cities can't be quarantined in time?
        What if the pollen can't be re-gathered,
        since pollen – as flowers have discovered –
        is easier to distribute than to collect?
        What if some processes are irreversible?
        What if the fart won't go back in?

But then I looked at the base pairs again
and I saw their actual atoms,
their carbon and oxygen and hydrogen.

And I saw a bigger problem on a smaller scale
    because if I can sew a button on a shirt
    then a machine can make a machine
    a thousand times smaller than itself
    which can, in principle, do the same
    until there are machines
    that can stack and shuffle individual atoms like Lego;
    can squirt into the world substances so new
    that no law has ever been framed to stop them;
    can make froglet-making froglets
    making froglet-making froglets like themselves;
    can super-oxygenate the blood of soldiers;
    can connect a nerve cell to a computer chip
    and operate an insect like a toy plane;
    can scatter tiny cameras like handfuls of grain,
    smart dust to broadcast the movements
    of secret armies or secret lovers.

And when I saw atoms being manipulated like that,
when I saw nanotechnology,
I thought: That's so cool
    but what if it *does* work?
    Because now that the armies of the Empire
    have surged against all before them,
    then whose soldiers will be supercharged?
    Who will breathe in the nanoparticles
    while working in the cosmetics factory?
    So that whose skin can be pampered?
    And who will be in the call centre,
    having spreadsheet software uploaded
    through their optic nerves,
    when the great powers of the world
    have the powers of gods?

And then I saw that what at first looked
like a paradoxical combination
of escapist science fiction and alarmist dystopianism
was in fact a paradoxical combination
of venture capitalism and state-funded research and development.
I saw billions of dollars spent in a single year,
American billions, military billions.
I saw that Nanotech is the new Apollo.
I saw that Down is the new Up.
I saw that the Molecule is the new Moon.

And I saw the protests starting already:
Hands off our atoms!
No patents on matter!
No nano, no nano, nano, nano, no!

And I looked a thousand times closer
and I saw the nucleus of a single carbon atom
lost inside the vastness of its electron shells
like a walnut kernel in a desert.

And I looked a thousand times closer
and I saw a particular proton in the nucleus
with nothing holding it to the other protons
but the raw strength of a permanent nuclear explosion
pressing inwards.

And I looked a thousand times closer
and I saw the proton's ingredients, its elusive quarks
with their mysterious fractional properties
of colour and flavour and spin and charge.
And then I saw that nanotechnology
is just the thin end of the wedge.

Because when the wise old shaman announced that
the Earth rests
on the back of a giant turtle,
he was asked:
But Wise One, then what supports the turtle?
To which he replied:
My child, another turtle.

Whereupon he was asked:
Then, Wise One, what supports the second turtle?
And he replied:
My child, you can chill out,
it's not your problem and anyway
it's turtles all the way down.

This is but the beginning
of a long campaign of subatomic imperialism.

And so I looked a thousand times closer
and then a thousand times closer still
and then a thousand times closer than that
and then another thousand times closer
and a thousand times closer again
and then just a hundred times closer
until I saw the Planck length.

I saw the quantum uncertainty
by which things are as much there as not-there.
I saw matching pairs of particles and anti-particles
bubbling in and out of non-existence.
I saw something that looked a lot like foam
and, in amongst, trying to get a grip
on the shifting essence of matter,
the vacuous foundations of reality

(and taking advantage of the fact
that, on this level, beauty really is in the eye of the beholder;
that, in other words, indeterminacy is collapsed by the observer;
that existence is determined by appearance;
that either good or evil may be chosen;
that wave/particle duality
does what it says on the quantum wave packet
and that the smallest things there are
are nothings)

I saw cold, corporate fingers reaching out to own
the final smallest pixellation of the Universe.
And the bottom-most turtle looked me in the eye and said:
This is a private party
and if your name's not on the list,
you're not coming in.

Late Night Showing

I went to the cinema and it was quite good
but the Judi Dench character was moaning that
'I don't want to die alone'

then I went to an adaptation of Thérèse Raquin
and when the old woman said
'I don't want to die alone'
everyone in the theatre started nodding along.

Why don't they want to die alone?
What's so fucking sociable about dying?

If you're coming round, I'll crack open the spesh.
I might make spinach filo parcels.
I'll put on an interesting record from Niger.
And to add to the fun, I'll stay alive
the whole evening.

Conversely, if I was going to die,
I don't want my final moments to be occupied by
you crapping on about some idiot at work
you fancy but who's mucked you about.

So if I die you're not invited.
The party's off. There are no front row seats.
It's going to be a quiet night in,
so quiet, you could hear someone breathe.

False Consciousness

The audience silenced its phones and, somehow,
itself. We could hardly believe our luck,
like suddenly having tickets to the Beatles.
   And we loved the ancient radical till *I don't*

   care who they sleep with, they don't
   need to stick it in our faces. His legend gave him
   not a higher standard but a free pass
   to sing for no one else's freedom

      and I felt the crowd turn like starlings
      (how does that work?) and I felt the turning
         turning me, like when music plays you.
      Or why the termites ate a floor.

There is washing machine learning,
   the sales guy said you don't tell it
how long to dry for, its sensors tell you,
it dries and wears the trousers.

   Language is the space between people,
   collectively incredulous at the lazy spite
      of heroes. The meaning's kind of clearer for
      structure, rhyme and metaphor,

      thoughts are imitations of talking.
         Year Three made their numberline
      by groupwork; like Lennon and McCartney,
         the whole isn't just the sum of (first order)

but is actively wiggling some of its parts.
Minds are made up of subroutines so
   sometimes I can't make up my mind.
I'm free to choose, it's just coincidence

    that the choice is always vinyl.
    Machines aren't as self-aware as monkeys,
only as much as lemurs. They can plan
but they can't detect unfairness,

     not reliably, not in aggregate
   (though it's what the Internet is for).
      My disabilities mean you have to keep it
      simple: red paint or blue? Unlike the peahen

who doesn't choose, in that she can't resist,
   the most compelling tail. A student
dressed in crochet stood up, swore at him,
   the past and also monogamy,

    and he knew he'd lost the room.
    Wasps think you're the picnic bully.
    The nest is restless, the class conscious,
      the greatest fans, the first to walk out.

    Don't complain about the traffic; you
      are the traffic. The markets are jittery,
      the age spirited, the joint jumping,
   and the band is the creation of the audience,
    whose phones woke up, to reconnect.

Countertransference

deteriorating situation in the east of the country
soldiers entered the village they
deliberate means of terrorising rival ethnic groups
   it's quarter to three in Trincomalee
   ten o'clock in Vladivostok
   and just before bedtime in part of Herts
     inside the radio are never not at war
     listening is an act
     two churchmen from the Republic of X
       one said it's important to remain neutral
       get both sides round the table
       feel their stories are heard

the president is a very stable genius
important to be non-directive
passive bystander who allowed
   subliminal subvocal subgestural prelinguistic
   microcues so you may begin to blame yourself
   for herding the trades unionists into the stadium
     Schadenfreudian and world authority
     on countertransference who said you were
     a manipulative little thing who made up
       victim victor witness
       barrel bombed the hospital
       but I'm not allowed on the couch

it's just coming up to the top of the hour
and it's very much not tea time
in crop failure province
    we've not been there for him
    and he is lost and we feel weird
    about all our non-acts
        the other one said our people
        are being skinned alive on the table
        and just need their stories to stop
            always the same old news
            the solemn voices are comforting
            like rain on the bedroom window
                when you think you're safe

Taxa

Homo sapiens named the animals
but Linnaeus named *Homo sapiens*
and while sorting the world into boxes
within boxes dropped the elephant into his Order Brutae
with anteaters and hippos,
in retrospect not a natural group,
there was no common ancestor without other descendants.

A category is a theory of relatedness
which is a theory about the past,
so abandoned categories are not maps of vanished countries
but of countries never there,
not the Soviet Union but El Dorado.

Anyway, someone removed anteaters
and that left the Order Pachydermata,
though thick skinned mammals are also
in retrospect not a natural group.

And classifications themselves fall into groups
of which the phylogenetic is just one
but all ideas are categories
with instances to which they don't apply,
instances that are not krill, pedantic or nesting.
If this were not true we'd only need one word:
Chunter Chunter
Chunter Chunter Chunter Chunter,
so all thought is taxonomy,
a Linnaean exercise in
the local government of the plant and animal kingdoms
whose suborders, infraclasses and superfamilies
are the shires, ridings and wapentakes
of a new biological superstate
with deranged Eukaryotic commissioners
bent on classifying and reclassifying

the caramel as a vertebrate,
the spidercrab as a fruit of the sea,
the otter as a great hairy tadpole,
and the future, eventually, as the past.

There are no longer any Quadrumana.
Four-handed Primates are not a natural group
without the addition of the two-handed
Bimana or people.

The Order Raptores, the flesh eating birds?
Sorry, finches and sparrows are miniature hawks
who went vegan for January and never went back.

And there's no Phylum Schizophyta, a group of microbes
almost but not quite coinstantiate with the Bacteria.

There is a whole zoo of moribund zoology,
of jargon degenerating into gibberish,
Ameridelphians for all American marsupials,
Unguiculates for all mammals with claws,
Thallophytes for algae and fungi,
groves of obsolete botany rotting to mulch;
this is the constant danger for all words,
that their corresponding taxa might be emptied of purpose
and stand revealed as just arbitrary
collections of stuff.

And Linnaeus, who
having invested so much in Latin names
at least had the decency to latinise his own,
floats about in some binomial afterlife,
eternally debating the problem of whether the set
of sets that don't include themselves
includes itself.
Chunter Chunter, he says,
Chunter Chunter Chunter.

Categories

(Joaquín Torres Garcia, *Constructivismo Universal*)

twenty in all
('Luz', a pear and a teapot)
(line graphs and faces)
(a fish, an ammonite and 'ano')

('Mundo', a spade, a hammer and a star)
using a spade and a hammer,
a world is constructed of nothing but starlight
and the lines drawn on the universal piece of old plank

(an ankh, a crucifix, an eye and a division sign)
(a heart, a sword, a Bunsen burner)
a tree has its own category
so does a spoon

Bird Flu as Meaning

There are, it is said, canine virtues:
loyalty, territoriality, obedience,
which even if actually vices
are still admirable in their doggedness.

In contrast, the feline virtues are independence
and furry sensuality asleep in the warmest spot,
while mice have a murine resourcefulness
that turns smallness into a subtle power.

Foxes have a vulpine cunning, hens a flustered
gallinity and owls a strigine pomposity.
Stags are noble, turkeys are gullible
and the big bad wolf is always ferocious.

Ground sloths and moas, if they still lived,
would mean something, that's why
we painted woolly rhinoceroses
on the cave walls but we

have factory farmed nobility,
performed toxicology tests on loyalty,
and in dark sheds of feathery panic
incubated a whole new creature.

We've performed a unsettling cave magic,
by imprisoning so many parts of ourselves,
the parts that want to bark at all strangers
or ruminate or snuffle, and we've liberated the one virtue

of the virus: blind ravenous virulence.

Please rush me Popey's nonsense factpack NOW

They called me mad but I'll show them.
Yes, it's me Pope Peter II,
one and only chronological tourist
turned quantum pontiff of metababble
from the 31st century, so really I should say:
they'll call me mad but I'll be going to have shown them.

The unchanging doctrine of the church has, er, changed,
because being infallible means never having to
state your premises, and now stands for
ONE: natural aristocracy with a title for everyone;
TWO: an end to capitalism, speciesism,
        motorised transport, boredom and misery (within reason);
THREE: an end to reason.

I reject the tiresome Popperian position
that rationality is a guarantor of liberty,
this argument may sound logical,
but then it would, wouldn't it?

I also reject creationism,
my church was built on the rock of ages
not the rock of just the other day
but reason has brought us nothing but deductions
about billions of years of geological time
within which reason itself flickers in but a fraction of a moment.
Why should it care about more about AD 2012
than about AD 5,000,000,012?

We can only outwit such
infinitesimalisation of our own existence
by rethroning the arbitrary
through the doctrine of transnonsense and ultimately
the abolition of time itself.

In the 31st century it is widely recognised that higher primates
and (oh go on then) medium primates too,
must be treated like famous scientists because
they're new people who've only just thought of themselves;
that some meanings have similar words,
which is no coincidence, in and of itself;
that reincarnation and time-travel together mean
that there might only be one person in the Universe
so you might as well be nice to yourself;
and that similarly butterflies are an immensely complicated
jigsaw
that has never quite solved itself.

In the 21st Century you had a pope praying for rain
on the balcony of Saint Peter's.
Yes, just like it says in the Bible,
assuming there's some other Bible.

Obviously the rain-praying pope of the twenty-ohs
was one of my agents obeying secret retro-chronical instructions
to do his best to make religion
look like the sterile mule-foal of literacy and superstition
belying the ongoing claim of the Christians
to be in fact the sweaty merger of virginity and mysticism.
But that's the kind of operation
you have to run when you're Pope Peter II,
high ultra-doge of transnonsense.

Now, transnonsense isn't transcendent transensical transience –
it's incandescence incarnate and I'm not exaggerating,
if anything I'm endaggerating.
Transnonsense isn't the absence of prescience,
the presence of nescience
nor the conscience of omniscience.
So don't buy the Great Decept
that it's more of a noncept than a concept,
it's been pre-emptively nontraceived
and I should know – I've had dinner with them.

When you enter the building, your nonsense factpack
can be perceived at the perception desk.
It's bigger than the quintessence of dialectics,
it's fatter than the octessence of pentalectics gone polynomial,
for I am Pope Peter II,
astrologist, psychologer, theologue, ideologian,
Christist, Marxite, Thatcherian.
My new disproved Buddhianity
will persuade trilobites to become ammonites,
motorists to renounce motorism,
Trappists Parkinsonism, and vice versa.
I've thrown away my old-style pope-type hat
in favour of a purple papal paper Christmas cracker crown.
I want curly magician slippers
like Suleiman the Magnificent's favourite jester
and a high collared cloak like Doctor Strange.

In me the church reaches its culmination and its negation.
It fulfils its purpose only through its destruction,
like a firelighter to the flames of genius.
I am its apogee, aphelion and apotheosis,
its furthest point from Earth, Sun and God.

I'll take the politics out of geopolitics.
And then I'll take out the geo as well
leaving nothing but a kind of lunar communism,
proving once again
that Anarchism is just Anarchy rebranded
to sell better in Waterstones
and that in the final triumph of deep geology over
the revealed concealment of concealed revealment,
that schist and schism will be preconciled.

I went to the bookies the other day
and I put a tenner on the meek
to inherit the Earth.
The odds were so good
that if I win –
I'll inherit the Earth.

Slogans to the People.
There's no future in Nihilism.
That's weird: I was just thinking about synchronicity too.

So my advice to you all is
to fill in the invisible form at the bottom of this poem
and tick the box saying:
Yes, please rush me Pope Peter the Rock's nonsense factpack NOW
or perhaps you already will.

Monomolecular Film

OPENING SCENE
AD 2000
A thirtysomething me, on stage in a downstairs pub room off the Essex Road. I'm winding them up, I'm going:

'...DNA took 20 years from its structure being discovered, to its sequence being altered. 20 years, ladies and gentlemen, from Crick and Watson and Franklin and so on, in 1953, to genetic engineering. And now it's said that our cells die, that *we* die, because our telomeres wear out, the little twists of DNA at the end of each chromosome. What do you reckon, another 20 years to sort that one out? Let's be generous and say it'll take till the year 2030. Then subtract a normal human lifespan and that means no one born after 1960 will have to die.'

Unsurprisingly I'm heckled by a 45 year old. So I say:

'Why are you so angry? Because you're going to die? Which you knew. Or because we're going to live? Which seems, well, churlish.'

FLASHBACK
Meanwhile thousands of years earlier:
The great king Gilgamesh, who is more perfect than any man, and the wild man Enkidu are celebrating their victories over the ferocious Humbaba, guardian of the cedars, and over the Moon Goddess and her Bull Of Heaven (all religions are contained within this moment, as forests are contained within their genes). They roar with joy:

'We have beer and we have dancing girls. Nature itself lies tamed in our timberyards. What can defeat us now?'

The answer is, of course, death. Death takes Enkidu. Gilgamesh weeps, then goes on a quest for immortality, which will need storyboarding. He has many adventures, most of them caused by his own stupidity. He finds the forbidden herb that gives endless life but the snake steals it away. Gilgamesh returns to his city, Uruk, to its gates of cedar. He says:

'These cities will spread across the Earth and that will be my immortality.'

FINAL SCENE
AD 2004
The Underworld. It is gloomy.
A ferryman splashes in the background.
Gilgamesh sits beneath poplar trees reading Earthly newspapers to three blind gods. He picks up a broadsheet which reports the news about Francis Crick with the headline:

'Man Who Discovered Secret of Life – Dead.'

FADE OUT

The Missing Term

How much did I miss you?
I missed you by a certain amount, μ.
And as time has been conjectured to heal
then, where μ_I = how much I missed you at first
and where t = time
elapsed since our final conversation at the bus stop,
it initially seemed that

$$\mu = \mu_I e^{-Ct}$$

with C being the rate of convalescence
and e the base of natural logs.

A large value of C would mean that μ would drop rapidly.
The curve would be asymptotic,
never reaching zero but becoming negligible,
lost in the background noise of everyday anguish.
It remained only to determine C's value.

But as the empty monochrome weeks
hauled themselves past my eyes like sick elephants,
I realised that μ was not diminishing at all.
μ was increasing.

*

I remember the beautiful theory of heat death.
Not death *by* heat, death *of* heat,
the eventual slowing down of all energy,
at a rate so utterly gradual that it placed Now
in the opening moments of creation,
so that when the Universe is a billion times older,
it would still be in its first bright youth.

I thought we were at the very beginning.
I thought we'd just left college three days ago
and that we were stepping out
into the shocking day of adulthood
with a pile of popular science books
to read on the train.

Only fourteen billion years old,
I thought we'd hit a hundred billion, a billion billion,
but all the time, everything was expanding
and the dark energy that was expanding it,
was growing secretly stronger.

I conjectured therefore that $C < 0$.
That must be why people get back together.
They don't heal, they grieve more and more.
But I knew you weren't coming back
(especially after the incident with Edwin's cardigan).

μ can't increase indefinitely, I thought,
weeping my way through a chapter
on the conservation of charismatic megafauna,
you never see old people who can't collect their pensions
for crying over a hideous break-up in 1929.

μ has to peak at some point,
the equation must have another term.
I reasoned that I didn't miss the end of the relationship,
I missed the good bits which ended $t + 1.5$ years ago;
that I was also relieved
that the recriminations were over;
and that it was this relief that was declining
from its initial state R_I at a rate D so that

$$\mu = \mu_I e^{-C(t + 1.5)} - R_I e^{-Dt}$$

with C and D having values such that the relief
initially faded more rapidly than the pain,
causing the overall value of μ to rise, temporarily.

I couldn't face Violet's party so
I drank white port in the bath and
looked inside my heart for approximate values of C and D
and the ratio between R_I and μ_I.

Then, differentiating with respect to t
I found its value when

$$\frac{d\mu}{dt} = 0$$

I'd found the turning point,
it was going to be the day before my birthday
that things would start to improve,
a discovery I immediately wanted to share with you,
which only made me miss you more
and in doing so demonstrated that my equation
was incomplete and that further research was needed
in the challenging field of comparative relationshiptology.

*

I began to see further problems with the model,
additional variables which were not orthogonal to μ,
like ω, the extent to which I worried
that you were in a similar kind of torment;
ϕ, the fear that you might not be;
and ψ, my growing ability to cope
with everyday decisions even as μ rose.

And then, at least according to the Scientific American,
there was the problem of dark energy,
of a cosmic sunderer leering
out of data gathered from exploding suns.

Because it followed from Hubble's Law

$$v = H_0\, d$$

that finding the velocities, v, and distances, d,
of variously ancient supernovae would reveal
the inconstancy of the constant rate of expansion, H_0,
of the spaciousness of space, and so measure
the deceleration of a flighty cosmos.

But the news was this:
H_0 was not diminishing at all.
H_0 was increasing.
The expansion was accelerating
and I missed you even more;
there was a missing term, a heartless levity, λ,
which could outweigh the cheap gravity
of the intergalactic deeps. Certain extrapolations showed
this energy growing and growing over time, t,
overwhelming the forces holding
planets to their orbits
and rocks together as planets.

Even the rubble will be reduced to dust,
the dust to a fine vapour,
at which point there will be several minutes to spare
before the irreparable moment
when the graph becomes an asymptote,
when darkness defeats the forces holding
the parts of atoms together. After which

there will be nothing.
Twenty two billion years in the future.
I'd thought the Universe was in its tender infancy
but considered as a human being,
time itself is already nearing thirty,

assuming the extrapolations to be accurate. If not,
the Big Rip might arrive sooner,
say, in the middle of Violet's next party,
shredding her guests into their constituent protons
and casting them apart at near light speed
across the formless void, a development
which would not increase the value of μ
and would not, therefore, trouble me one iota.

The Book of Kelp

A snowflake can be melted by a breeze
  but is stronger than a train.
Water flows humbly to the lowest place
  but erodes mountains as it trickles.
A bough can be broken by the wind
  but kelp waves in time with the current.

The song flows out of the wren,
  which cannot be seen among the leaves.
The bat hears its way in the dark
  on wings that make no sound.
The seedling flows towards the sun
  and the sun never ceases its song.

The pack paces and snarls
  but fangs do not frighten the gnat.
A mouse falls from a gable,
  too slight to be hurt by height.
No one would name a raindrop
  but oceans are made of nothing more.

Better than Paradise

for Yassin Ali Omar

Your error scaling up the recipe,
your ratio mistake, exalted me,
the day you detonated and announced
that 'God is Great' then looked around to see

a tube train on a Thursday afternoon,
not paradise lit by a crescent moon.
You taught me wings can reasonably rise
from fertile falsehood and from the cocoon

of woe I left among the smoke and heat
and heels abandoned under Warren Street.
I bought a watermelon walking home,
a whole green world, irrational and sweet.

Notes

Black Sites
The pianist in the third verse is Dmitri Shostakovich and the episode is related in his (alleged) memoir *Testimony*.

The Book of Kelp
Prompted by a particularly geological line from Chapter 78 of the *Tao Teh Ching*: 'Nothing in the world is softer and weaker than water; But for attacking the hard and strong there is nothing like it!' (translated by John C.H. Wu, Boston, Mass.: Shambhala, 1990).

Embryo Concepts
Audrey Hepburn's bookshop in *Funny Face*.

Knickers on Frogs
Lazzaro Spallanzani, eighteenth century Italian physiologist.

Mission Creep
The veteran in Auden's *Roman Wall Blues* deserves a happier ending.

Our Chairman
Some readers may recognise the source of the italicised lines.

The So-Called Individual
The italicised lines are all from Rudolf Virchow, nineteenth century German pathologist and politician.

Taxa
The point about ex-raptors refers to: Jarvis, E.D. et al., Whole-genome analyses resolve early branches in the tree of life of modern birds, *Science* 346 (2014), p.1320-1331.

Turtles
Since writing this I keep seeing references everywhere to the fact that there are turtles all the way down. My starting point here was Carl Sagan's version of the story in *Broca's Brain* (New York: Random House, 1979) combined with the wonderful short film *Powers of Ten: A Film Dealing with the Relative Size of Things in the Universe and the Effect of Adding Another Zero* (1977), also known as the Eames Movie after its makers Charles and Ray Eames.

5.4 Million
The figure is from the International Rescue Committee's 2008 report *Mortality in the Democratic Republic of Congo: An ongoing crisis.*

Acknowledgments

Thanks are due to the editors of the following publications where versions of some of these poems were first published: *Broadsheet, Interalia, The Nail, Red Pepper,* Todd Swift (ed) *Babylon Burning,* Claire Fauset (ed) *This Poem Is Sponsored By,* Todd Swift (ed) *Future Welcome* and BBC Radio Four's *Word of Mouth.*

Others were included in *FLOW – the Cancer Day Unit Art Project,* a collaboration with Heather Barnett, at Guy's Hospital, London 2010 and in the exhibition *Small Worlds,* a collaboration with Heather Barnett at the Museum of the History of Science, Oxford, 2007.

Special thanks to Heather Barnett for showing me how to turn work into play and vice versa.

Special thanks also to Sophia Blackwell without whose relentless encouragement and inspiring poetic example this book would not exist.